Junior Science Book of
Icebergs
and
Glaciers

By PATRICIA LAUBER

Illustrated by Evelyn Urbanowich

SCHOLASTIC BOOK SERVICES

NEW YORK · TORONTO · LONDON · AUCKLAND · SYDNEY · TOKYO

The author and editor are grateful to the following who read the manuscript of this book and advised on its content: Miss Agnes Creagh, Publications Director of the Geological Society of America, and Captain R. L. Mellen, U. S. Coast Guard.

JUNIOR SCIENCE BOOK OF ICEBERGS AND GLACIERS is one of the books in the *Junior Science Series* published by Garrard Publishing Company, Champaign, Illinois. Other Junior Science books available in reinforced library bindings from Garrard Publishing Company are:

Junior Science Book of

Bacteria	Pond Life
Beavers	Rain, Hail, Sleet, and Snow
Big Cats	Rock Collecting
Electricity	Seashells
Elephants	Sound
Flying	Stars
Heat	Trees
Light	Turtles
Magnets	Weather Experiments
Penguins	

8th printing ·· March 1973

Printed in the U.S.A.

Contents

Iceberg Dead Ahead!

THE DATE was April 14, 1912. The place was the North Atlantic Ocean. And the proud new ship was named *Titanic*. She was the biggest passenger ship in the world. She was the fastest. And she was called the safest. "The *Titanic* cannot sink. She is unsinkable," her owners said.

Now the *Titanic* was making her first voyage. Three days earlier she had left England, bound for New York. Her owners expected her to set a speed record. And it looked as if she would. The weather had been fair, the sea calm. The *Titanic*'s powerful engines thrust her through the ocean.

April 14 was a fair, mild day. The *Titanic* sped on toward New York. But she was also speeding toward danger. For each mile brought her closer to a certain part of the North Atlantic. Every spring this part is invaded by hundreds of icebergs — floating mountains of ice.

At noon the first warnings came in. Ships ahead radioed news of icebergs that were in their paths.

The *Titanic* sped on.

Night came, cold and clear. The *Titanic* rushed through the dark. Another ice warning was received on the ship's radio.

The *Titanic* churned ahead. Her lookouts

peered into the night. Ship's bells rang the hour — 11:30 P.M.

Silently a great, gray, ghostly shape loomed up ahead. A lookout saw it. "Iceberg dead ahead!" he cried.

The *Titanic* swung to the right. She slowed down, trembling with strain. But she was traveling too fast to stop.

Ship and iceberg shouldered each other. A crunching sound echoed the length of the ship. Tons of ice chips rained onto her decks.

Below deck, floods of water were pouring into the *Titanic*. Ice had ripped a huge gash in her steel side. The proud new ship was sinking.

At 2:15 A.M. the great ship shuddered. Her bow dipped under the water. Her stern rose high. Five minutes later the *Titanic* sank. With her went some 1,500 people.

A few hours later dawn came. Survivors

saw the iceberg glittering in the early light. Its blue-white ice showed no scars.

The iceberg bobbed gently, drifting away with the current. It was heading south. And there it would melt.

Now it was hard as rock. Rock-hard, it had sunk the unsinkable ship. But soon it would melt. For a mighty iceberg is only ice. It must obey the same laws of nature as all other ice.

Small Ice and Big Ice

ICEBERGS are huge. They tower above the water. They weigh millions of tons. Yet in some ways an iceberg is just like an ice cube from your refrigerator. The reason is simple. They are both ice.

Ice is frozen water. It is water in a solid form—one of the three forms water takes. You find all three forms in your kitchen.

Open a faucet, and water runs out. This is water as a *liquid*.

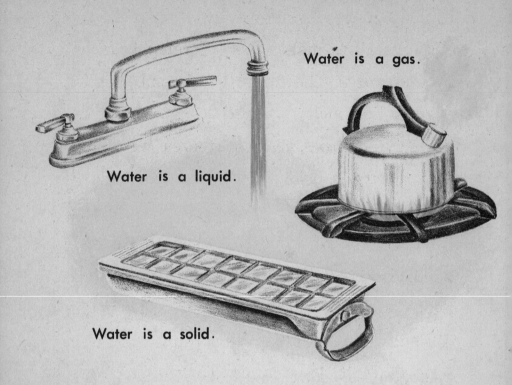

Water is a gas.

Water is a liquid.

Water is a solid.

Boil a kettle of water, and steam forms. This is water as a *gas*. When the steam meets the cooler air, it condenses into a cloud of tiny water droplets.

Fill an ice tray with water and freeze it. The ice is water as a *solid*.

You can easily change the solid back into a liquid. Put the ice cube in a warm place. Soon it will melt. Then you have water again.

Temperature makes the difference between ice and water. The figure to remember is 32 degrees. Ice melts when the temperature is above 32 degrees. Water freezes when the temperature is below 32. We call 32 degrees "the freezing point" of water.

What happens to water when it freezes? The liquid changes into crystals. The crystals are locked together in a solid mass. This is ice.

When water freezes, something else also happens to it. It expands. That is, it grows larger. It takes up more space.

Fill an ice tray to the brim with water.

Ice crystals

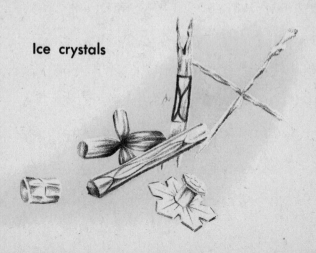

Freeze it. Then look at the ice. It has risen above the brim of the ice tray. The ice takes up more space than the water did. But the ice and the water weigh the same. Water expands when it freezes, but it does not grow heavier.

The trays of ice and water weigh the same.

Now suppose you have two ice trays. They are exactly the same. You want to fill one with water and the other with ice. You want to fill them both to the brim.

It's easy to fill one tray to the brim with water. But how can you fill the other to the brim with ice? Here's how. You fill the tray with water, but not to the brim. You leave a little room for the water to expand as it freezes into ice.

This time water and ice take up the same space. But they don't weigh the same. You put more water in one tray, so it is heavier. The tray with ice is lighter.

When it takes up the same space as water, ice is lighter than water. Because it is lighter, ice floats in water. An ice cube floats in a glass of water. And an iceberg floats in the sea.

Place an ice cube in water. Notice how it floats. Most of it is beneath the water. The

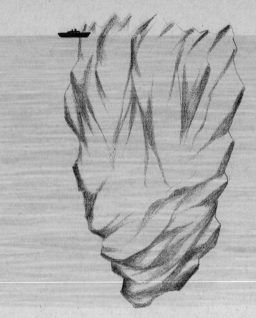

Only a small part of an iceberg shows above water.

same thing is true of an iceberg. Most of it is hidden. Only a small part rises above the water.

So in several ways an ice cube and an iceberg are alike. Both are frozen water; they melt when the temperature rises above the freezing point. Both are made of crystals locked together; they are rock-hard. Both are lighter than water; they float.

But there is one big difference between an ice cube and an iceberg. They are not formed the same way.

An ice cube is made by freezing water. It is made when liquid changes into a solid. An iceberg begins as snow, and snow is water gas that is frozen.

A rain cloud carries water in its gas form. We call this water *vapor*. Freezing temperature can change the water vapor to snow.

Snow falls in fluffy flakes. Each flake is a feathery crystal. New-fallen snow is light, airy, and soft.

Perhaps you have seen what happens to snow on a sidewalk. In early morning the snow is a feathery blanket. Then people begin to walk on it. Their feet pack it down. Flakes are crushed together. Their lacy points break off. The snow is no longer feathery. It is solid and hard. People go on walking over it. The snow melts a little. Then it freezes again. Soon the snow is like ice.

The ice in an iceberg formed from packed-down snow. But people had nothing to do with it. Iceberg ice formed in far-away places where few people go. Icebergs are pieces of the earth's "big ice," which we call glaciers.

Malaspina Glacier, in southern Alaska

How the Big Ice Formed

Long ago in the far, cold places of the earth, great snows fell and piled up. In those cold lands, the summer sun could not melt all the snows of winter. Each year more snow fell than the sun could melt. And so the snows built up, layer upon layer. Over a very long time, they grew hundreds of feet thick.

Heavy ice covers the sea at the North Pole.

The great weight of newer snows packed down the old snow into rock-hard ice. And then it forced the ice to move. Under this great weight, the ice flowed slowly forward.

In that way, the earth's glaciers formed. The glaciers are huge masses of flowing ice. The ice formed from snows that fell during hundreds of years. This big ice is found in many parts of the world.

An icecap hides the land at the South Pole.

Glaciers lie among the peaks of lofty mountains.

Great glaciers hug Arctic lands. These are called *icecaps*. An icecap is a broad mound-shaped mass of ice. A huge icecap hides much of Greenland. Big and thick, it covers mountains and plains alike.

A giant icecap grips Antarctica. In places, this ice is almost two miles thick. Its weight has pressed down the whole continent. Once Antarctica was the highest land in the world. Now large parts of it are below sea level. The ice has pressed Antarctica into the earth.

Glaciers don't lie still. They flow slowly downhill or outward toward the sea.

A mountain glacier flows down toward the valley. It flows until it reaches an area where the air is warmer. Here the ice melts.

An icecap flows outward from its center. That is its highest, thickest part. There the weight is greatest. The weight pushes the ice from the center outward in all directions. And so the ice flows toward the sea.

From Greenland and Antarctica fingers of ice reach out into the sea. After a while, they break off and float away. These pieces are then called icebergs.

Antarctic icebergs are the world's biggest.

Icebergs break loose and float out to sea.

Many are a mile or two long. Explorers have found some twenty or thirty miles long.

These giants do little harm because few ships go near Antarctica. The icebergs simply drift away to warmer waters and melt.

The dangerous icebergs come from Greenland. These are the ones that drift into the North Atlantic.

Part of Greenland's thick icecap

A Silent, Ghostly Fleet

ALL WINTER, snows fall in Greenland. All winter, ice grows. Bit by bit, the ice flows forward. It reaches out in great fingers of ice that are hundreds of feet thick.

Heavy and long, the fingers of ice push out into the sea.

Then spring comes. This is the time when icebergs are born. They are born as ice fingers break off.

Big ice breaks with a mighty crash like thunder. The roar echoes up and down the Greenland coast. A newborn iceberg plunges through the water. Up and down and over it goes. Its plunging churns the water. Waves rise. The air is filled with spray.

Finally, each iceberg finds its balance. It settles in the water. The sea grows calm around it. Water pours off the surface of the ice.

Each spring about 16,000 icebergs are born in the water off Greenland. They come in many shapes and sizes.

A small iceberg is big enough to fill a football field. A big one would cover two city blocks. A giant iceberg may be a mile long.

Some icebergs are flat-topped, like great cakes of ice. Most are topped by jagged peaks that tower hundreds of feet above the water. These look like fairy castles. All are made of blue-white ice that glitters in the sun.

Bobbing and gleaming, the new icebergs drift in the sea. First they are pushed about by winds and tides. Then they are caught in an ocean current.

An ocean current is a steady flow of water. It is broad, deep, and strong. It is like a river running through the sea. In the Atlantic Ocean there are many currents.

One current sweeps down the east coast of

Greenland. Each spring thousands of icebergs are caught in it. Carried along, they form a silent, ghostly fleet.

The big white fleet sails south to the tip of Greenland. A current carries it around the tip. Then the fleet heads north.

The fleet itself moves in silence. But the air is filled with the booming thunder of many more icebergs being born along the west coast of Greenland. By the hundreds they join the fleet.

A long voyage lies ahead. It is a voyage that covers 5,000 miles — north, west, and south. Slowly drifting, an iceberg takes three years to make that trip.

The fleet travels north, following Greenland's shore. At Cape York, it swings west across Baffin Bay. It passes the tip of Ellesmere Island. There it turns again. Now it is heading south.

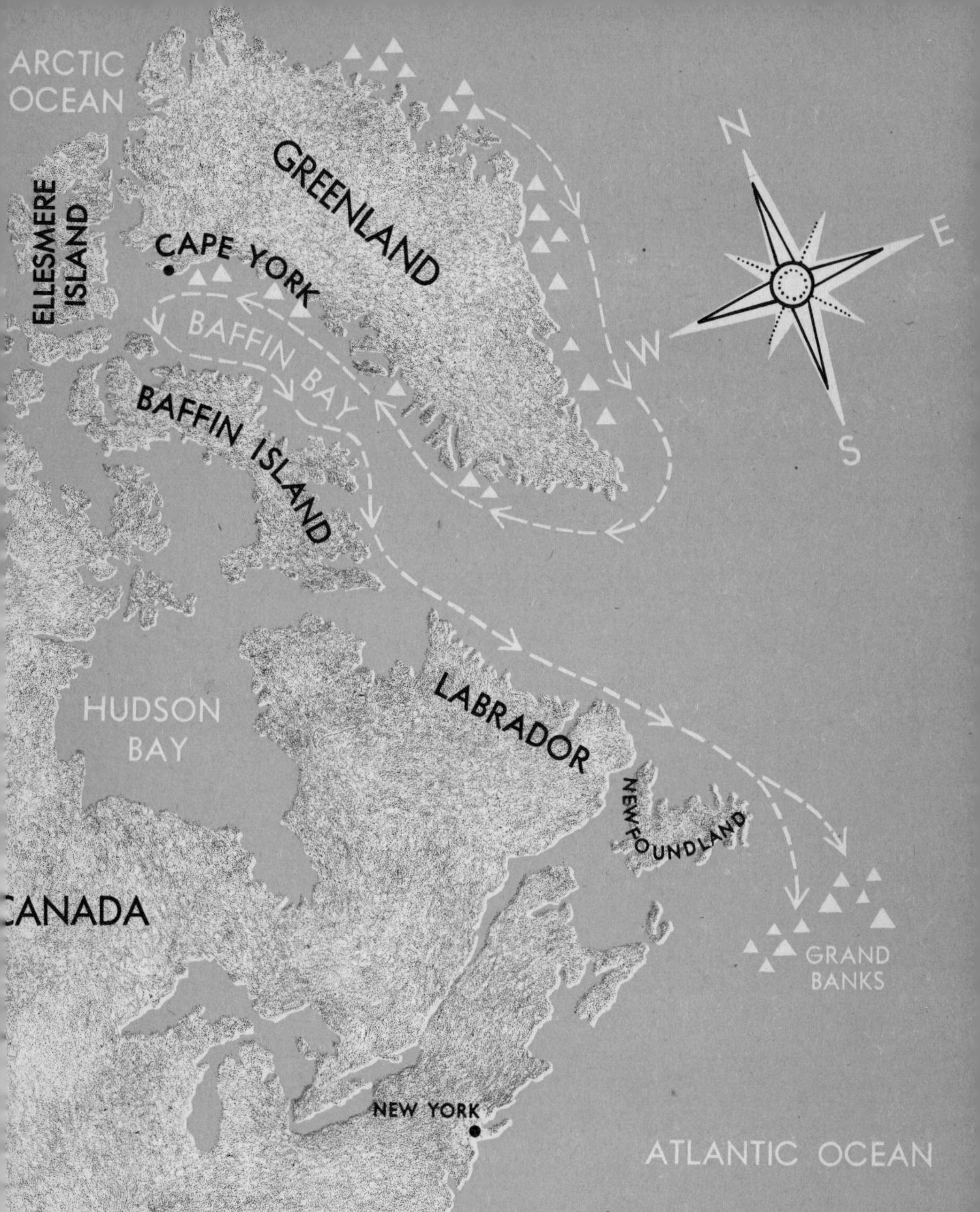

ARCTIC
OCEAN

GREENLAND

ELLESMERE
ISLAND

CAPE YORK

BAFFIN BAY

BAFFIN ISLAND

HUDSON
BAY

LABRADOR

NEWFOUNDLAND

CANADA

GRAND
BANKS

NEW YORK

ATLANTIC OCEAN

N

E

W

S

Icebergs break off the Greenland
icecap and form a great white fleet.
The current carries them along the
course marked by the arrows and
white dotted line.

By this time the fleet is much smaller. Many of the icebergs have been lost. Some have run aground. Some have been captured by other currents and have drifted away into northern coves. There they lie trapped, their voyage ended.

Many more icebergs will be lost on the 2,500-mile trip south.

Slowly and silently the fleet floats past Baffin Island. It passes Labrador, then Newfoundland.

South of Newfoundland, the fleet scatters. It scatters over a shallow area of sea called the Grand Banks.

Now the big icebergs are nearing the end of their voyage. Soon a warm current will seize them and melt them. But first they will cross the Grand Banks.

Many ships also cross the Banks. This is the danger area for ships. Here the *Titanic* struck an iceberg and sank. Here many ships before her went down. Here the sea bottom is littered with the bones of men and ships.

The Grand Banks lie on the shortest shipping route between northern Europe and North America. It is the busiest shipping route in the world.

So here the silent, ghostly fleet is watched and tracked by men of the Ice Patrol.

The End of
a Long Story

THE SINKING of the *Titanic* shocked the world. Over the years, many ships had been sunk by icebergs. But the *Titanic* was the biggest and most famous. Suddenly people realized how dangerous icebergs could be. Something had to be done to protect ships.

And soon something was done.

The ships of many nations sailed the North

Atlantic. These nations held a meeting. They decided to set up an ice patrol. Each would pay a share of the cost. The United States Coast Guard was asked to do the patroling.

Every spring Coast Guard cutters sailed toward Newfoundland. The cutters had a big job. They were to find icebergs and warn ships. In cold and rain and fog, the cutters tracked the icebergs. They did their job well. Ice has never sunk a ship there while the Ice Patrol was on guard.

Cutters still do this job today. But now they have help. Planes also patrol the area. They tell the cutters where to look for icebergs. Weather satellites are starting to help, too. Their cameras can photograph the area. But the main job is done on the sea.

A cutter sails up to an iceberg. Crew members make a study of the floating ice mountain. They note its size and shape. They

A Coast Guard cutter sails among the icebergs.

find out where it is drifting. They measure
the speed at which it drifts.

These facts are radioed to headquarters in
Newfoundland. There the Ice Patrol keeps
track of all icebergs in its area. From there
warnings are sent out to ships.

Some years 1,100 to 1,200 icebergs invade
the Grand Banks. Other years there are almost

no icebergs. Usually about 400 icebergs scatter over the Banks.

Few or many, all must be tracked by the Ice Patrol. The work begins in early spring and goes on into July or August. It ends only when all the icebergs have melted. Until then they must be tracked and watched. Man has found no way to destroy them.

The Coast Guard has tried to destroy icebergs by shelling them with big guns. It has attacked them with torpedoes. It has dropped fire bombs on them. Nothing works. Each time there is a loud bang. A cloud of steam rises. Splinters of ice fall into the sea. But the big, hard icebergs sail on.

Icebergs have only one real enemy. This is the warm current called the Gulf Stream. It seizes icebergs near the edge of the Grand Banks. It carries them along and bathes them in waters as warm as 68 degrees.

An iceberg cannot last in warm water and warm air. Soon it begins to change. Its surface softens, then melts. Streams of water run off its sides.

Sun, wind, and water work on the ice. The sun beats down on it. Wind and water

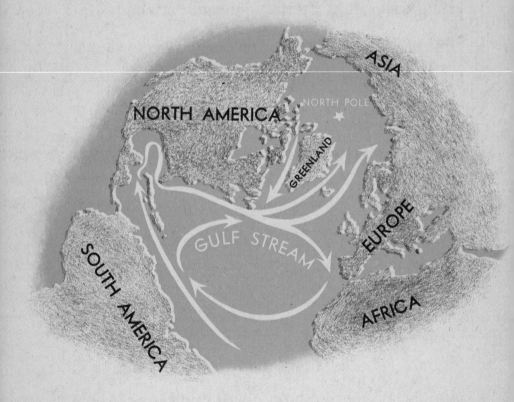

White arrows mark the route of the Gulf Stream.

eat away at it. The ice becomes soft and spongy. Great chunks of it break off. The chunks melt. And in just a few days the mighty iceberg vanishes.

The end of the iceberg is the end of a long, long story. For this was ice that formed a thousand or more years ago.

In that far-away time, winds swept the ocean and picked up moisture. The moisture fell as snow in Greenland. The snow did not melt.

Hundreds of years passed. The snow was packed into rock-hard ice. It became part of Greenland's icecap.

Still more time passed. The ice flowed slowly toward the sea. Reaching the sea, it broke off and floated away.

In three years the iceberg traveled 5,000 miles through the water. It weathered Arctic blizzards and gale winds. It beat its way through packs of sea ice. It was so hard that man could not destroy it.

But in a few days the Gulf Stream melted it. The ice changed to water. And the water went back into the ocean.

Sun and wind and warm water melt the iceberg.

Water
Locked
in Ice

THE EARTH has a huge amount of water. Water covers seven tenths of the earth's surface.

Most of this water is in the oceans. A small part is in lakes and rivers. A tiny part is in the air. About one one-hundredth is snow and ice.

"One one-hundredth" of the earth's water —that doesn't sound like very much. Yet it is a great deal of water.

Locked up in ice, that water makes all the

earth's glaciers. And glaciers cover one tenth of the earth's land.

Glacier-covered land is far away from most of us. But its ice affects all of us.

For example, take the mountain glaciers. They are small as glaciers go. Yet many people depend on this ice for water. Their water supply comes from melting glaciers.

Or suppose all the big ice melted at once. The water it holds would flow into the oceans. The ocean levels would rise 200 feet. Huge pieces of coast would vanish under the oceans. Big cities would be drowned.

Or what if glaciers grew greatly? They would grow if more snow fell on them and did not melt. The moisture for this snow would come out of the oceans. The water level of each ocean would drop. There would be new coastlines. Great seaports would become inland cities.

Mountain glaciers supply water to streams and rivers.

Glaciers are important to us. Changes in glaciers make big changes in life on earth. And at times glaciers do change.

There have been times when glaciers grew and grew. The ice reached out and spread over green lands. It reached out until it covered one third of the earth's land. For thousands of years it held the land in an icy grip.

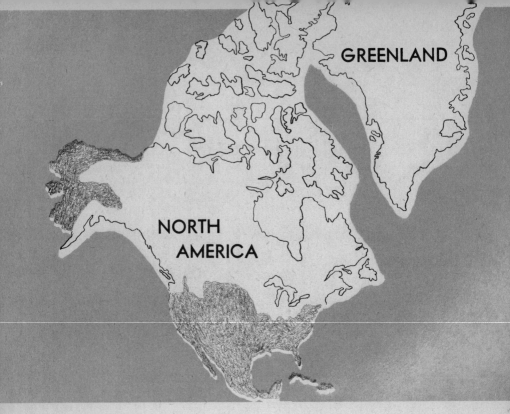

GREENLAND

NORTH
AMERICA

Glaciers once covered the area shown in white above.

Those times are called the ice ages. The last one began about a million years ago. It is the one we know most about. And we call it the Ice Age.

The Ice Age had four stages. Four times the great glaciers reached down. Four times they melted and drew back. They drew back

ASIA

EUROPE

AFRICA

Ice Age glaciers covered part of England and France.

to the places where they lie today.

Why did the glaciers grow? Why did they melt back? Will they grow again? No one knows for sure.

But this we do know. An ice age is a cruel and fearsome time. It is a time of long and terrible winter.

The Ice Age: A Time of Ever-Winter

THE GREAT ICE AGE did not begin as a huge blizzard. It did not suddenly sweep the earth. It did not cover green lands with white overnight.

The Ice Age began slowly. It began in the far-away places where glaciers lie today. It began as snow that fell and did not melt.

On Antarctica a giant icecap grew. But its touch was not felt by other lands. Antarctica is surrounded by ocean. And glaciers do not form on water. They are land ice. Antarctica's ice broke off and floated away as icebergs.

Elsewhere, on lofty mountains, great glaciers grew. They reached down into the valleys.

On northern lands, thick icecaps piled up. The ice began to flow south. Foot by foot, the ice crept toward green lands.

Its front edge was a giant wall of ice. In some places the wall was a mile high. The great weight of the icecap pushed this wall forward. On, on it went. Nothing could stop the advancing ice. It covered hills, plains, lakes. It tore away parts of mountains. It crushed whole forests. It dug into the ground and scooped up boulders, dirt, gravel.

A cold white sheet of ice lay heavy upon one third of the earth's land. Greenland was gripped by a huge icecap. Northern Europe was covered by a vast sheet of ice. Ice lay thick on parts of Russia, Siberia, and Asia.

In North America, ice reached down over Canada and into the United States. Its high wall stretched from coast to coast. It reached south into what we now call New Jersey, Missouri, and Nebraska.

Where there was ice, all else vanished. There was only ice — cold, thick, lifeless. Ice that glittered in the sun. Ice that crunched forward, scraping, grinding, scouring. Ice that sent its wintry breath far ahead.

In the path of this ice all living things fled or died.

Four times the ice came down. Four times it melted and shrank back. The last time it drew back was 10,000 years ago.

The melting ice left behind great floods of

water. In time, the water ran off the land into rivers and seas.

The ice also left the land much changed. Ice had carved the sides of mountains. It had dug out valleys. It had built some hills and torn down others. It had snatched up rocks and dirt from one place and dropped them somewhere else. It had made islands.

Today we can see great rocks which were moved into place by glaciers during the Ice Age.

Its floods of melted ice had made new rivers and lakes.

For a long time this land was still. Then life came slowly back to it. From the south, plants spread north. Animals followed the plants. And the kinds of life had also been changed by the ice.

Some kinds of plants had vanished from the earth. They had grown before the Ice Age came. Now they grew no more.

The same thing was true of certain animals. A million years ago, there was a beast called the saber-toothed tiger. Big and fierce, this tiger ruled wherever he lived. No other animal was his match. But his kind died out during the Ice Age. How did this happen? No one knows.

The end of the mammoths is even stranger. The mammoths were huge animals of the

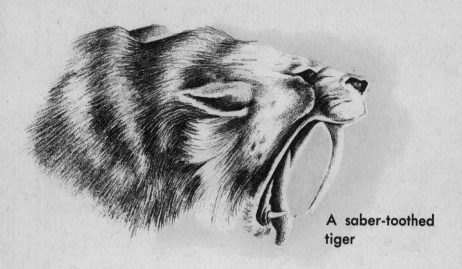

A saber-toothed tiger

elephant family. During the Ice Age, some became cold-loving animals. Their fur grew long and thick. It protected them against the cold. These mammoths did not flee south. They lived near the ice. But when the ice melted, the mammoths died out.

The mammoths had changed once. They had learned to live with the cold. Why couldn't they change again? What happened to them? Again, no one knows.

Other animals vanished only from certain

places. Elephants, camels, and horses are three of those animals. A million years ago, herds of elephants lived in North America. So did camels. So did horses. By the end of the Ice Age, none were left in North America. But they did still live in other lands.

We know little about the men who lived during the Ice Age. But we do know that there were people. They were simple, early people who lived in caves. On the walls of their caves, they drew pictures of animals.

Some of these people must have seen the ice. They must have felt the cold winds of ever-winter. But these people could not write. And so they left no record of the Ice Age or of the great floods.

In time, the land was free of ice and floods. It was green and fruitful again. Men came

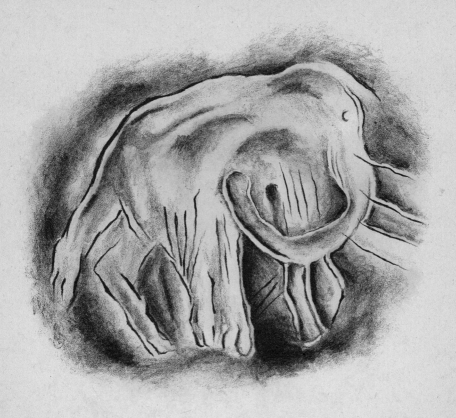

Cave men left pictures of the early mammoth.

to live on it. They hunted and farmed. Hundreds and hundreds of years went by. Men built towns and cities on the land. But for many, many years no one guessed the secret of the past. No one guessed that this green land had once been white.

Secrets of
the Big Ice

THE GLACIERS had drawn back. They had drawn back to the mountaintops and to northern lands. There they lay, holding their secret. Behind them they had left clues. They had left their mark upon the land. But for a long time no one knew what the clues meant. The Ice Age remained a secret.

Scientists first discovered this secret 150

years ago. Working like detectives, they pieced together the clues. They learned to read the marks that ice had left on the land. And they learned what had happened. There had been a time of ice, a time of ever-winter.

But the big ice also held many other secrets. Over the years, many scientists have tried to discover these secrets. And they are still trying today.

Some scientists are studying the ice itself. They live and work on the great icecaps and mountain glaciers. There are many things they want to know about the ice.

For example, no one knows how ice flows. How can rock-hard ice flow? Do changes take place in its crystals? What kind of changes are they?

Scientists look for answers in the ice. They take samples from different depths. They chop some from the surface. They drill deep into

A scientist drills a core of ice from a glacier.

the ice and bring up a core. They climb down
into great cracks. There, 200 feet down, they
take more samples. Then they study all the
samples. How are they alike? How are they
different?

Other scientists are measuring the flow of
glaciers. They want to know: How fast do
glaciers move? Does each glacier always move

at the same rate? Which glaciers flow fastest?

Answering these questions takes time. Scientists must measure glaciers in many parts of the world. They must measure the glaciers for many years.

Some scientists are digging into the past. They are asking: Has the climate changed in the last thousand years? How much snow fell in Greenland a hundred years ago? Four hundred years ago?

No written records answer these questions. Our weather records do not go back far enough. But scientists have found a "deep freeze" of weather history. It is in Greenland's icecap.

The icecap is made of layers of ice. Each layer formed from snow that fell in one year. The layers are something like the growth rings in a tree.

Scientists drill into the icecap. They take

out a big core of ice. Then they study its layers. The layers tell them about snows that fell hundreds of years ago.

In such ways scientists are prying secrets out of the big ice. What they learn helps still other scientists. These men want to know: Are we at the very end of the Ice Age? Or will the great glaciers reach down again?

A scientist lowers himself into a crevasse to study the walls of a glacier.

Will the Ice Come Again?

TODAY most glaciers are shrinking. They are melting and becoming smaller.

Big snows still fall in winter. The snows pack down into ice. In winter the glaciers grow.

But in summer glaciers melt more than they used to. More ice melts in summer than forms in winter. And so the glaciers shrink.

There is a reason for this. The climate has been warming up. Part of the Arctic is ten degrees warmer than it used to be. Parts of Antarctica are five degrees warmer than they used to be. Water runs off the glaciers into the oceans. And ocean levels are slowly rising.

What does all of this mean? Is the last of the big ice melting away? Is the Ice Age really over?

Scientists used to think so. They did not know what had made the Ice Age start. But they were sure this was the end of it. The climate was warming. Glaciers were melting. In time the ice would melt away. The earth would be free of glaciers.

Today many scientists have changed their minds. They still do not know what made the Ice Age start. But they believe it has not ended. This is what they say:

In the Ice Age there were four times when glaciers grew. There were four times when glaciers melted. The fourth melting time is still going on. We are living in it.

Many scientists believe that some day this melting time will end. Then glaciers will grow again. They will reach down for the fifth time.

Why will glaciers grow? They will grow because the Arctic Ocean has warmed up. They grew in the past for the same reason.

That sounds like a strange reason. But it makes sense when you understand about the Arctic Ocean.

It is a small ocean. And it is the only ocean that freezes over. Every winter it freezes, much as a large lake does, because it is nearly surrounded by land. Only a little warm water can get into it from the south.

The little warm water comes from the Atlantic. The two oceans meet between Norway and Greenland. But they do not mix much. The place where they meet is shallow. It is

The two oceans meet between Greenland and Norway.

like a giant doorsill which keeps the two oceans apart. Normally, only a little water gets over the sill.

But suppose the climate warms a little. Water melting from glaciers pours into the oceans. The Atlantic and Arctic oceans rise. They rise high above the sill. The two oceans begin to mix more.

Cold water from the Arctic Ocean pours into the big Atlantic. Warm water from the Atlantic Ocean pours into the small Arctic. The Arctic Ocean becomes much warmer. It no longer freezes in winter. Instead, it is open water.

Winter winds sweep over this open water. They pick up a lot of moisture. They pick up much more moisture than they did when the ocean was frozen.

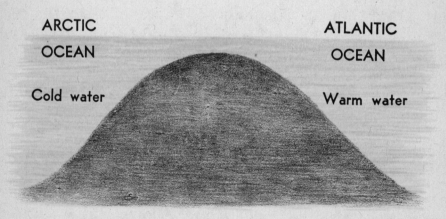

ARCTIC OCEAN

ATLANTIC OCEAN

Cold water

Warm water

The place where the oceans meet is like a giant doorsill. It keeps the oceans from mixing together.

The moisture-filled air blows over Arctic lands. The Arctic lands are cold. So the moisture freezes and falls as snow. The snowfalls are huge, and they make the glaciers grow greatly. For it is not intense cold that makes glaciers, but great snows that the summer sun cannot melt.

The glaciers grow and push south. Heavy snows go on falling. The glaciers grow and grow. Again they spread over green lands. Again they hold these lands in an icy grip.

As long as great snows fall, the glaciers grow. But in time the great snows must end. There is not enough water left for heavy snows.

A huge amount of water is now locked up in ice. This water has come out of the oceans. So the ocean levels are much lower. The Atlantic and Arctic oceans no longer mix freely. The Atlantic is not warming the Arctic Ocean.

Glaciers
melt.

Snowfalls
are small.

Ocean levels
rise.

There is less moisture
in the Arctic air.

Atlantic Ocean warms
Arctic Ocean.

The Arctic Ocean
freezes over.

The Arctic no longer
freezes in winter.

Ocean levels
drop.

There is more moisture
in the Arctic air.

Much water is locked
in ice.

Snowfalls are heavy.

Glaciers
grow.

The Arctic Ocean again freezes over in winter. Winds sweep its ice. They pick up much less moisture. So the snowfalls are smaller. More snow melts in summer than falls in winter. Glaciers are no longer growing. They are shrinking.

The big ice draws back once more. It melts and melts and melts. As it melts, ocean levels rise. And then the whole cycle happens again.

Was that what happened in the past? Is that why ice reached down four times? Two American scientists believe so. They have found clues that seem to prove it. Many other scientists agree with them.

Suppose they are right. What will happen in the future?

First, the big ice will keep melting. Oceans will rise. Great floods will pour over the land. You may see the start of these floods during your life.

A few hundred years will pass. Flood waters will draw back. Oceans will start to drop, for in the far places glaciers will be growing. They will grow and grow, fed by heavy snows.

They will grow until they spread over much of the earth's land.

What if these scientists are wrong? Then now may well be the end of the Ice Age. All the glaciers will melt away. Oceans will rise greatly, but there will be no growing glaciers.

At present, there is no way to tell about the future. We can only wait while scientists probe the secrets of the earth's big ice.

Index